D1743601

This fascinating new book presents a unique idea which will certainly capture the imagination of young adults. It is a concise and entertaining introduction to the art of astrology, and focuses mainly on the attributes and characteristics of people whose sign of the Zodiac is Cancer (June 22 - July 22). You will learn the basics of astrology and understand how the stars influence your character, talents, relationships with other Zodiac signs - in fact, every aspect of your life!

If you want to know what your future holds, you don't have to stare at the stars in the sky - simply take this book and find out for yourself.

Amanda Starr, a practicing astrologer, has published several books on the subject of the stars, the planets, and their influence on our lives.

This series contains twelve books, each describing one of the twelve Signs of the Zodiac. Look at the chart (page 72) to find your special book, according to your date of birth.

Amanda Starr

ASTROLOGY
FOR YOUNG ADULTS

My Sign is
Cancer

Astrolog Publishing House

Astrolog Publishing House
P.O. Box 1123, Hod Hasharon 45111, Israel
Tel: 972-9-7412044
Fax: 972-9-7442714
E-Mail: info@astrolog.co.il
Astrolog Web Site: www.astrolog.co.il

© Amanda Starr 1999

ISBN 965-494-066-3

Published by Astrolog Publishing House 2000

Printed in Israel
1 3 5 7 9 8 6 4 2

Cancer

GETTING INTO ASTROLOGY...

Since prehistoric times, people have believed that the stars influence their lives, and that their fate was sealed the moment they were born. The exact time of each person's birth has a particular place on the astrological birth map. This map shows the position of the planets at the moment of your birth, and accompanies you throughout your life. An astrologer who analyzes your birth map will be able to tell you about your character and your life up to now, and give you a pretty good idea of your future. The birth maps of different people can be compared to see if they are compatible in romance, business, and so on.

The following elements are the basic components of the birth map, as used by professional astrologers:

All twelve signs of the Zodiac

All ten planets

All twelve houses

A large number of aspects (the angles formed between the planets, as seen from Earth).

Astrological birth maps are different than one another because the planets are in different positions. Each birth map is unique. It is a kind of secret language based on astrological codes. To understand the birth map, astrologers decipher these codes by looking at the position and combination of the planets and aspects at a specific moment.

The planets are quite close to the earth, and move in fixed orbits around the sun. As far as astrology is concerned, the millions of stars in space don't move. They form a kind of fixed background for the planets. As the earth moves round the sun, a different part of the starry background comes into focus each month. In

the starry backgournd, you can see groups of stars. Astrologers gave names to twelve groups of stars, which together are called the Zodiac, or Wheel of Fortune. This is the belt of the twelve star formations, or constellations, surrounding the earth. The sun "moves" from one constellation to the next, and remains in ech one for about a month. Whoever is born when the sun is in a particular constellation belongs to its sun sign. The sun sign is the most important component in the astrological map, and this book focuses mainly on the sun sign.

In addition to the sun, astrologers must identify the position of each of the planets and aspects, and how they fit into the map. These have their own symbols and powers, and all these things influence the birth map.

The number of combinations, intersections and meeting-points between the different elements of the birth map are infinite, and these are important for understanding the map, for analyzing a person's personality, and for predicting the future. At the moment of birth, the sun may be in any one of the twelve signs of the Zodiac and in any one of the houses in the astrological map.

As we said before, the sign in which the sun is located at the moment of birth is called the *sun sign*, and it often becomes the most important sign in our birth map. This sign shows us how our basic potential and our creative talents will develop. Remember that the analysis of the personal signs in this book is based on the sun signs.

The twelve signs of the Zodiac each have special and unique physical and psychological characteristics.

The strength of these characteristics in each one of us depends on how they interact with the other elements in the map.

How do we know which sign we belong to? Well, the most common form of astrology focuses on the sun signs. Sun signs define the basic energy that influences each one of us to be

what we are and do what we do. The place on the chart where the sun appears tells us our sign of the Zodiac. For example, if you were born on a date when the sun was in Scorpio in the astrological map, your sign is Scorpio, and you are influenced by the energy of Scorpio. It doesn't matter if the moon and all the other planets were in other signs at that time.

The horoscopes that you read in magazines and newspapers are based mainly on the sun signs and very little on the influence of the other planets. By dividing the world's population into twelve groups, according to the date of birth, they predict the future of the world's population for the coming week, month or year!

Now, if horoscopes make this twelve-part division, you might be wondering how come all the people born under a particular sign aren't the same either in looks or in character. Let's face it, that would be pretty boring! The answer is that the sun sign is not a fixed, unchanging piece of information, but rather a whole "menu"

of characteristics ranging from positive to negative. This means that all the people born under a certain sun sign share this "menu'," but just like a menu in a restaurant, where we choose only a few items, each person has *some*, not all, of the characteristics. That's why people who belong to the same sign can be very different from each other.

You must also remember that the person's nature and characteristics only become fixed and stable during his twenties. As a young adult, you should consider horoscopes and astrological maps as general directions rather than as an exact picture of a fixed, unchanging state.

If you want to foretell your future, you need a personal birth map showing all the exact data that have been calculated according to your precise moment and place of birth. However, the sun sign – the sign of the Zodiac – on its own gives a lot of information about your personality and characteristics. If an astrologer also takes the position of the planets and the location of the different houses into account, a lot more can be discovered about you.

In addition, each sign can be divided into three parts (as you'll see later on), and this produces a more detailed analysis. Another thing is that the characteristics of each individual day of the year can be determined; they should be added to the characteristics of the sun sign to make the analysis more accurate.

Astrology involves the flow of energy and making choices. If something negative appears in the map, we have the choice of quitting or coping with it. The map will give us an indication of what the problem is, and what we can do to put things right, but it is up to us to do it.

The important factors
in analyzing the chart are:

1. The signs of the Zodiac: These signs are divided into four categories, according to the elements of fire, water, air and earth.

On the following pages is a summary of every sun sign and its characteristics:

> *** Sign * Dates * Ruling Planet ***
> *** Element * Characteristics ***

Aries
March 21 - April 20
Mars
Fire

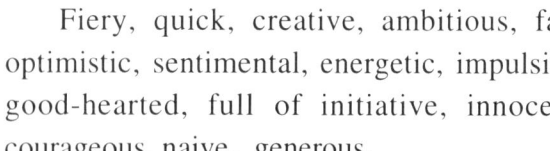
Fiery, quick, creative, ambitious, fair, optimistic, sentimental, energetic, impulsive, good-hearted, full of initiative, innocent, courageous, naive, generous.

Taurus
April 21 - May 20
Venus
Earth

Honest, frank, sensitive, logical, patient, esthetic, artistic, practical, stable, efficient, independent, organized, intuitive, good with money, down-to-earth, sociable.

Gemini
May 21 - June 21
Mercury
Air

Energetic, friendly, helpful, flexible, tactful, intellectual, artistic, curious, articulate, good with money, independent, intuitive, crafty, sparkling.

Cancer
June 22 - July 22
Moon
Water

Sensitive, nature-loving, straightforward, shy, home-loving, persevering, diplomatic, compassionate, tolerant, defensive, organized, tidy, independent, family-loving.

Leo
July 23 - Aug. 22
Sun
Fire

Courageous, brave, worldly, energetic, dignified, regal, self-centered, charismatic, powerful, loyal, self-confident, ambitious, dramatic, outspoken, generous.

Virgo
Aug. 23 - Sept. 22
Mercury
Earth

Curious, intelligent, critical, cool-headed, practical, serious, perfectionist, discriminating, efficient, precise, conservative, methodical, choosy, witty, fussy.

Libra
Sept. 23 - Oct. 23
Venus
Air
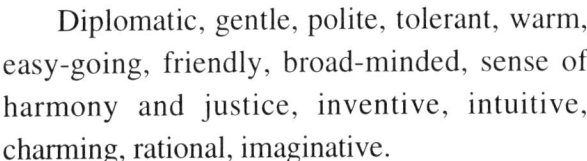

Diplomatic, gentle, polite, tolerant, warm, easy-going, friendly, broad-minded, sense of harmony and justice, inventive, intuitive, charming, rational, imaginative.

Scorpio
Oct. 24 - Nov. 21
Pluto
Water

Ambitious, strong-willed, self-satisfied, influential, secretive, magnetic, intuitive, mysterious, intense, energetic, emotional, courageous, competitive, independent.

Sagittarius
Nov. 22 - Dec. 21
Jupiter
Fire

Developed sense of morality and justice, honest, forthright, intelligent, optimistic, tolerant, fair, open-minded, adventurous, humane, enlightened, generous, outspoken.

Capricorn
Dec. 22 - Jan. 20
Saturn
Earth

Practical, efficient, conservative, diligent, down-to-earth, logical, independent, shrewd, ambitious, responsible, stable, confident, serious, achievement-oriented.

Aquarius
Jan. 21 - Feb. 18
Uranus
Air

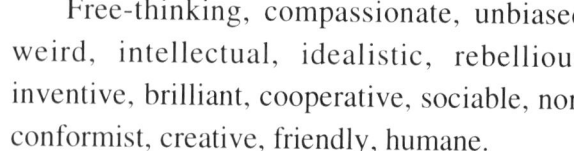

Free-thinking, compassionate, unbiased, weird, intellectual, idealistic, rebellious, inventive, brilliant, cooperative, sociable, non-conformist, creative, friendly, humane.

Pisces
Feb. 19 - March 20
Neptune
Water

Creative, sensitive, imaginative, spiritual, kind-hearted, introvert, romantic, emotional, self-sacrificing, soft, loving, compassionate, unique, intuitive, naive, charming.

2. The planets: Each planet has its own astrological characteristics.

Sun – The sun is the basic force that motivates us. It represents our conscious part, the direction of our development, and the basic values we believe in and

practice. If the sun is in a strong position, we will enjoy strong life energy, vitality, feeling of self, and the ability to express ourselves. The sun rules Leo.

Moon – The moon represents how we react to outside influences and the actions of other people. Our feeling of belonging and our  faith in our emotions depends on the position of the moon. The moon is responsible for our irrational, unconscious need to go with the flow of our basic life energy - or against it. It influences our home life. The moon rules Cancer.

Mercur... ...ury represents the ....ur thinking is influ...... ...sign of the Zodiac. It is responsible for our ability to communicate with people, to make decisions and to transmit ideas. It directs our creative forces. The sign where Mercury is located defines the knowledge that is important to us. Mercury rules Gemini and Virgo.

Venus – Venus is responsible for how we express our feelings in personal relationships, such as love and marriage. Venus' location tells  women how they see themselves and their ability to love. Venus reveals to men the kind of woman they find attractive. It also tells us about our attitude to money, property, love of comfort, and social values. Venus rules Taurus and Libra, and makes them especially sensitive to beauty.

Mars – Mars represents how we express our ambitions, and how we try to make ourselves noticed. In a fire sign, Mars indicates assertiveness. In an air 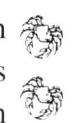 sign, it indicates the ability to speak well and the patience to explain. When Mars is in difficult aspects, anger and impulsiveness dominate us. The location of Mars tells men how they see themselves. In women, it shows assertiveness, and reveals the kind of man she finds attractive. Mars rules Aries.

Jupiter – Jupiter indicates our attitude to social, moral, philosophical or religious opinions and issues. Its location tells us what we will do in order to feel secure, and if we are able to communicate with a superior force. It also indicates how giving we are toward society, how we receive help and support, and how we relate to those less fortunate than ourselves. Jupiter rules Sagittarius.

Saturn – Saturn represents restraint and self-discipline. Its location indicates how much responsibility we are prepared to undertake, as well as our maturity and self-discipline. It also tells us what we'll do professionally, and if that suits us. We may

— **24** —

have to overcome obstacles, or change things in our personality in order to succeed. Saturn represents the areas in which we find order, stability, status and respect. Saturn rules Capricorn.

Uranus – Uranus indicates our need for liberty and individualism. It also shows how we link up with universal knowledge, which is the source of  original ideas, inspiration, understanding of life, and the ability to solve problems. Its location reveals the motives behind our aspirations, hopes and goals. Uranus rules Aquarius.

Neptune – Neptune's location indicates how we reveal our mystic potential. It also shows why certain people have supernatural powers. Neptune

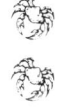

helps us serve others unselfishly. Our ability to form images is influenced by its location. It shows us what will be influenced by our dreams, and reveals the supernatural and powers of intuition. Neptune rules Pisces.

Pluto – Pluto's location shows us in which area of life we must make changes in ourselves and our surroundings. Pluto indicates how the fate of mankind in general will link up with our individual fate. Its location shows how we will be exposed to mysterious things. Pluto rules Scorpio.

3. The houses: These are the twelve two-hour segments that together make up the day's 24 hours – the time it takes for the earth to revolve once on its own axis.

The first house is most important, as it represents our self-awareness and reaction to external stimuli.

The second house represents the money we need to develop and support ourselves.

The third house represents our ability to think and communicate, our powers of intuition, and our intellectual reaction to our surroundings.

The fourth house represents our experience in domestic and family matters.

The fifth house represents our creative expression, and how we feel about the pleasures of life and children.

The sixth house represents our attitude toward work and service, our ability to do important jobs and think in a practical way.

The seventh house represents our ability to form relationships with other people, and reveals how others relate to us.

The eighth house deals with scientific subjects such as nuclear physics and theoretical math, as well as mystical and extrasensory things.

The ninth house deals with philosophy, religion, law, social consciousness, and institutions of higher learning.

The tenth house represents professional or public obligations, status and reputation, and our attitude toward business or political power structures.

The eleventh house represents our ability to communicate with groups and organizations, and how we go about implementing universal ideas.

The twelfth house represents our mental health, our emotional reactions, and our habits.

4. **The aspects:** These are the angles that are formed between the planets, as seen from Earth, and are measured in degrees, minutes and seconds (like trigonometry).

Opposite Signs

It is very important for you to know the characteristics of the sign that is your polar opposite in the Zodiac, since the good points of the opposite sign are often the very things that you have to work on in yourself. Here are the things that each sign should try and learn from its opposite sign:

Aries should learn from *Libra* to be less selfish, and to try and understand other people's feelings.

Taurus should learn from *Scorpio* how to view reality less superficially and even a bit mystically.

Gemini should learn from *Sagittarius* how to develop a broad, philosophical point of view.

Cancer should learn from *Capricorn* how to be more independent and cope with hassles.

Leo should learn from *Aquarius* how to get down to a mere mortal's level without thinking that they are going down in the world.

Virgo should learn from *Pisces* that it is possible to help others out of love, sympathy and empathy.

Libra should learn from *Aries* to stand up for their principles and to be an individual.

Scorpio should learn from *Taurus* how to enjoy a simple, uncomplicated life by living in a calm, stable way.

Sagittarius should learn from *Gemini* that a light-hearted, simple, uncommitted attitude has a lot of advantages.

Capricorn should learn from *Cancer* that values such as love, warmth and affection are sources of enormous power.

Aquarius should learn from *Leo* how to present their original ideas to society in a respectable and impressive way.

Pisces should learn from *Virgo* how to prevent people from taking advantage of them.

The sun in the signs

As we said before, the sun sign is very important in the birth map. However, besides the sun sign, there are other influencing factors that are significant. The sign that is rising on the horizon must be taken into account, and so must the aspects and the signs and houses in which the most influential planets (Moon, Mercury, Venus and Mars) are located. A person whose sun is located in a particular sign is influenced by the characteristic energy of that sign, but this refers to a typical member of that sign. The more supporting signs there are on the map, the stronger the properties of the sign become. The properties of the sign can also be weakened by signs that oppose or contradict it.

Now that you have an idea of how astrology works, it's time to look at your sign in detail, to see what kind of person you are, how you relate to others, the best professions for you, who your perfect partner is, and more...

Here is a place for your photo.

Before we turn to the analysis of your personal sign, why don't you fill in the following charts and questionnaires so that you will have more information about yourself, your friends, and your family. People will probably love to tell you about their sign of the Zodiac.

Remember, if you know a person's date of birth, you can use the chart on page 72 to find the correct sign of the Zodiac.

MY FAMILY'S "ZODIAC TREE"

My sign of the Zodiac is ....

My brothers' and sisters' signs of the Zodiac are: ....

My mother's sign of the Zodiac is ....

My father's sign of the Zodiac is ....

My grandmother's (on my mother's side) sign of the Zodiac is ....

My grandfather's (on my mother's side) sign of the Zodiac is ....

My grandmother's (on my father's side) sign of the Zodiac is ....

My grandfather's (on my father's side) sign of the Zodiac is ....

Look at your family's "Zodiac Tree." Is there any sign that occurs often in your family? Does your *opposite sign* appear in the "Zodiac Tree"? How well does your sign of the Zodiac fit into the rest of your family's signs?

MY SIGN

Cancer.

brother	brother	sister	sister
....	....	Aries	....

mother	father
Libra.	Gemini

grandfather	grandmother	grandfather	grandmother
Gemini	Leo	Tauras	Leo

MY FRIENDS

My sign of the Zodiac is .... Cancer

My friends' signs are:

Name: ...Jenni... Sign: ...Leo......

Name: ...Sarah... Sign: ...Cancer...

Name: ...Mat... Sign: ...pices...

Name: ...Lauren... Sign: ...Leo......

Name: ...Emma... Sign: ...Leo......

Does one of my friends have the opposite sign to me?   Yes / No

Who? ....

I can check out my relationship with my friend .... using astrology.

Up until now, you've learned about astrology in general. Now it's time to look at your personal sun sign.

CANCER:
JUNE 22nd - JULY 22nd

WHAT ARE CANCER PEOPLE LIKE?

On June 22nd, the sun says goodbye to Gemini, and moves into Cancer, a water sign whose symbol is the crab. Cancer is ruled by the watery and feminine moon. The main things about Cancer people are their shyness, extreme sensitivity, hesitancy, and dreaminess. They are easily hurt, and are afraid of looking ridiculous and being criticized; they are also anxious about all kinds of things, often lying awake at night worrying. They are real home-bodies, who love their homes and families. They are hungry for love and warmth, and are very romantic and sentimental. Because they are nostalgic people, they are interested in their roots and their family trees, as well as history, archaeology, religion, and tradition. They have fantastic memories, which help them in whatever they do. They respect rules and laws, and they love wandering around and exploring unspoiled, clean nature sites.

Cancer people can be moody, which means that sometimes they are happy, friendly, and outgoing, and at others they are withdrawn and sad. They are very tactful, and do not blurt out exactly what they are thinking. When their feelings are hurt, they become prickly, and it is difficult to get on with them. Cancer people are often hardworking, sympathetic, tolerant, and peace-loving, and adore their families. They do a lot for the community in which they live.

Because of their closeness to their families, they are ideal children to their parents and ideal parents to their kids. Their parental instincts to love and protect their kids are strong. They love cooking (and are good at it)

because it helps them express their need to love and take care of others. They can be so possessive of their loved ones that sometimes it is hard for either side to break free. They are particularly close to their mothers. In fact, there is little they do in life without consulting their parents. Anyone who gets involved with a Cancer person should take that into account, for better or for worse!

Although they love their families, and are happiest when they are with them, they don't really show it outwardly; as a result, people sometimes think that they are a bit cold. If someone misunderstands them, they become miserable, depressed and withdrawn. Although there are sometimes hassles in their lives, they overcome them with determination and patience.

They are very good at defending themselves and others. Their crab's shell is a defense mechanism that disguises their feelings and delicate nature. They defend themselves by hiding in their shells. They don't attack, but just refuse to act; passive resistance is their weapon. They do everything they can to protect their security, including their attachment to material things. Because of their trusting nature and their need for love and warmth, they can be taken in easily by sweet words and promises – and then get badly hurt. This happens over and over again, in spite of their wisdom and experience. Hey guys – isn't it time you started learning from your mistakes?

Cancer people are not particularly outgoing. They keep their worries, feelings and opinions to themselves, and don't like to be opposed.

Although they are fairly timid and sensitive, Cancer people are stubborn and quite capable of going after what they want, once they know what it is. Their powers of endurance are amazing. They are well-known for their precision, organization, tidiness and efficiency. They won't stand for people interfering in their affairs or projects, and insist on taking all the responsibility for them. They are very good at business, but their success is a result of hard work and refusing to give up, rather than taking risks and gambling. In fact, they are unsuccessful gamblers.

Not surprisingly, Cancer people have a deep love of nature and the outdoors, especially anything to do with water. This goes for their choice of professions as well. They are good at professions that are connected with liquids – bar owners, bartenders, liquor merchants, laundry operators, and hydraulic engineers. Naturally, they feel happy and comfortable at sea, and this means that they are good sailors and naval officers. Because they tend to become involved in the life of the community, public service also suits them. They make good government officials, social workers, politicians, hotel managers, and caterers. Literature and music, which go well with romantic and imaginative temperaments, are also good professions for them, especially if they mix with the public.

As far as their health is concerned, they must take care of the chest region. Sometimes, they have problems in that area, as well as with their stomachs. They should take care with their diets and try not to eat too much junk food. Goodbye, burgers and fries, hello salads and fish! They don't handle stress too well, so they should try to be calm.

The Zodiac opposite of warm, gushing Cancer, which is ruled by the mother figure of the moon, is restrained and self-controlled Capricorn, which is ruled by the father figure of Saturn.

THE THREE GROUPS OF CANCER PEOPLE

Now that we've seen the general characteristics of the sign, we can look at Cancer in a bit more detail by subdividing its people into three sections consisting of about 10 days each: June 22-July 1, July 2-11, and July 12- 22.

First group: June 22-July 1

These are typical Cancer people, and the influence of the moon on them is very great. This means that whatever is said and written about Cancer people in general is even more true for them. However, they are still partly under the influence of Gemini, the quick-thinking, flexible and unpredictable. The people of this group have extremely sharp memories – sharper than the other two groups, they take money and property very seriously, and they are economical to the point of being, er, for want of a better word, cheap.

These first-third Cancer people are very close to their families – especially to their mothers. They require huge doses of love and protection, and some psychologists claim that they really want to return to their mother's womb!

Second group: July 2-11

Although they are also true Cancer people, they are under the influence of Scorpio, too, and the vibes transmitted to them by the planet Pluto have to be diluted and blended.

These Cancer people enjoy physical love more than the other groups, and their relationships with other people are based on sex. They are the toughest and strongest of the Cancer people, the ones who are the least tied to home and family. Don't hurt their feelings, as they tend to bear a grudge and wait for an opportunity to get their own back. They are good friends, and can be wonderful partners. However, if they become jealous, watch out! See that the green-eyed monster doesn't poke his ugly head out.

Third group: July 12-22

These are true Cancer people, too, but they are also influenced by Pisces and the planet Neptune. These Cancer people are the most romantic and dreamy of all, and, as a result, also the most sensitive and easily hurt. They identify with other people's misery, and they behave in a sympathetic and understanding manner toward those around them. Most artists and intellectuals who are Cancer people belong to this third of the sign.

As you must realize, all this sensitivity, dreaminess and highly developed imagination often lead to confusion and embarrassment.

This means that these Cancer people are very moody, and feeling depressed is quite common with them.

SOME INTERESTING FACTS
ABOUT CANCER PEOPLE

Their lucky colors are emerald green, white, and silver, and their precious stones are emeralds, pearls, crystal, and moonstones. Their lucky number is 2, and their metal is silver. Cancer plants are saxifrage, tarragon, riverside plants, carob, lettuce, fleawort, cucumbers, and corn chamomile. Cancer animals include oysters, snails, and crabs.

The objects and things that are linked with Cancer people are silverware, cutlery, sailing vessels, handkerchiefs, beds, sheets, pillows, eggs, baskets, preserves, veils, muslin, pacifiers, honey, and jars.

Places and regions that are associated with Cancer are the muddy areas near water sources, shores, lakes, and pools of water. In the home, Cancer places are the kitchen and dining-room, the basement, and the area near the washing-machine. Cancer structures are hotels, restaurants, and residential buildings. Their countries are Scotland, Holland, Africa, Mauritius, Paraguay, and China, while their cities are Tunis, Algiers, Amsterdam, Venice, Bern, Milan, New York, and Stockholm. The direction of Cancer is north.

AND NOW FOR ROMANCE: WHICH OF THE SIGNS SUIT CANCER?

Cancer + Aries: Good for people who seek hair-raising adventures, provided that Cancer wants to get his or her kicks from doing things that SWAT teams do! Stay away from this one, and find someone more suitable.

Cancer + Taurus: Yeah! Especially for Cancer people belonging to the second group. Taurus' calm and practical nature suits Cancer very well, and inspires stability and tranquillity.

Cancer + Gemini: Nah – Gemini's lightness, speed and mischief aren't the ideal characteristics for Cancer, who is so withdrawn and easily hurt. Forget it.

Cancer + Cancer: Depends what they're expecting ... A couple like this could live in an isolated igloo at the North Pole and not miss having anyone around. Their main problem lies in their mood swings.

Cancer + Leo: A lot of fun for trips and outings, but watch out that the proud and conceited Leo doesn't suddenly eat Cancer the crab as an appetizer!

Cancer + Virgo: Real good. Could last for years and years. Virgo's fussy, hardworking, hygienic nature is exactly what our confused and sensitive Cancer needs.

Cancer + Libra: Think twice about this one. Neither of them is exactly the world's champion decision-maker, and their ship will lack a captain. Bring a compass, somebody!

Cancer + Scorpio: Freeze right there! This could be a problem. Scorpio's toughness and vindictive nature are definitely not what Cancer needs.

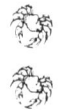

Cancer + Sagittarius: This is good for a nice cozy chat over a cup of coffee, but not more than that. Sagittarius' love of open spaces and freedom don't sit well with Cancer's home-loving and family-oriented nature. So stick to coffee...

Cancer + Capricorn: Awesome! Fantastic! Capricorn needs a warm, admiring, and responsive audience, and Cancer needs a serious, mature and understanding partner. This couple is custom-made.

Cancer + Aquarius: Only if there's no other choice. Chronically spaced-out Aquarius will find it difficult to come down to earth and give Cancer the love and warmth he or she needs.

Cancer + Pisces: Hmm, interesting. Both sides are sensitive and withdrawn, but both are capable of lavishing buckets of love and warmth on the other. It's worth a try. Worst comes to worst – they'll say a tearful goodbye.

HAPPY BIRTHDAY, CANCER! WHAT DOES YOUR SPECIAL DAY SAY ABOUT YOU?

June 22: You work hard, and you're successful.

June 23: You're a smart person, but you sometimes get into arguments with your family. Try to avoid this, and you'll be happier.

June 24: You don't often have money worries. Job offers come your way quite often.

June 25: You take things to heart, and sometimes feel unhappy. If you could be a bit more objective, things would be better.

June 26: You have a talent for writing. Go for it – success is on the horizon.

June 27: You take your friends seriously and follow their advice. You're a good friend to them, too.

June 28: You are very helpful, but sometimes undertake to do things that are too

57

much for you. Think carefully before taking on more responsibility than you already have.

June 29: Your love life is important to you, and you are serious about it.

June 30: You find it difficult to control your emotions. Make an effort, and you'll be surprised at the results.

July 1: You're not a person who stays in one place. Where there is money to be made, you go!

July 2: You are the kind of person who know how to deal with life's hassles.

July 3: Your life is generally peaceful, happy, and full of love.

July 4: You have very good friends, but sometimes you argue with them, and then make up. You love traveling.

July 5: You are the kind of person who is happy in love. You're smart, and this leads to success.

July 6: You are good at business deals. Traveling is something you do often.

July 7: You're a very honest person, and

sometimes you have to battle with your conscience a bit. However, you always reach the right decision.

July 8: You're very artistic, and succeed in professions where you can make the most of your talent.

July 9: You are an adventurous spirit who welcomes new people and places.

July 10: You have excellent intuition, which allows you to make the correct decisions.

July 11: Your family hassles you sometimes, but you know how to deal with them without getting upset. You don't have money worries.

July 12: There is a lot of happiness in your life. You know how to solve problems.

July 13: You are an excellent actor. As a result, fame and fortune are yours.

July 14: You know what you want in life, and you know how to get it.

July 15: You are a very friendly person who enjoys an active social life.

July 16: You sometimes quarrel with members of your family, but you make up soon afterward. You don't bear a grudge.

July 17: You are a sensitive person who is easily hurt. Try to develop a thicker skin, and life will be happier.

July 18: You were born to appear in public, and you'll be very successful. Money is on its way!

July 19: You don't particularly like changes, but if they come along, you try to get used to them.

July 20: Friends and love are very important to you. Just don't give anyone cause to talk about you behind your back.

July 21: You are an intellectual type, and this will make you successful. You know how to deal with changes in your life.

July 22: You're very helpful to other people, and your friends know how reliable you are. You are decisive.

Now that you've learned all about your sign, you can check yourself in the same way as an astrologer would analyze you. In the following pages, you will find questions that will help you draw conclusions from everything you have read up until now.

I was born on (date)*

...... June 28ᵗʰ 1986 ......

So my sun sign is

....

The planet that influences me the most is

.........., and the reason is ....

....

....

....

....

* If you were born on the first or last day
of a sign, you need to check your sun sign
according to your year and hour of birth.

I can clearly see the following characteristics of the planet .... in myself.

1. ....
   ....

2. ....
   ....

3. ....
   ....

4. ....
   ....

5. ....
   ....

I can see the following characteristics of the sun sign .... in myself.

1. ....
   ....

2. ....
   ....

3. ....
   ....

4. ....
   ....

5. ....
   ....

I can see the following characteristics of my third of the sign .... in myself.

1. ....
   ....

2. ....
   ....

3. ....
   ....

4. ....
   ....

5. ....
   ....

When I look at the characteristics of the day I was born, I think I have a:

large / medium / small

degree of ....

I think that I have:

strong / average / weak

characteristics of my sun sign.

Now that I know that my sign of the Zodiac is ...., and I understand the characteristics that I might have in the future, I want to find role models who have the same sign of the Zodiac as me.

1. Among the people I know personally who also belong to my sign of the Zodiac:

Name: ....

Date of birth: ....

This person would be a good role model because

....

....

....

....

Name:.....................

Date of birth: ....

This person would be a good role model because

....

....

....

....

Name:.....................

Date of birth: ....

This person would be a good role model because

....

....

....

....

2. Among the famous people I know about who also belong to my sign of the Zodiac:

Name:....................

Date of birth: ....

This person would be a good role model because

....

....

Name:....................

Date of birth:....................

This person would be a good role model because

....

....

Name:...................

Date of birth: ....

This person would be a good role model

because

....

....

Famous Cancer people:

*Millionaire John Rockefeller; authors
Ernest Hemingway, Franz Kafka,
Hermann Hesse, and George Orwell;
Alexander the Great; artists Marc Chagall
and Modigliani; Princess Diana; actors Yul
Brynner and Natalie Wood; Roman emperor
Julius Caesar; astronaut John Glenn;
Helen Keller; artist Rembrandt van Rijn.*

Aries	March 21 - April 20
Taurus	April 21 - May 20
Gemini	May 21 - June 21
Cancer	June 22 - July 22
Leo	July 23 - Aug. 22
Virgo	Aug. 23 - Sept. 22
Libra	Sept. 23 - Oct. 23
Scorpio	Oct. 24 - Nov. 21
Sagittarius	Nov. 22 - Dec. 21
Capricorn	Dec. 22 - Jan. 20
Aquarius	Jan. 21 - Feb. 18
Pisces	Feb. 19 - March 20